# Amazon Echo Show

## A Comprehensive and Well-Organized Guidebook to Experience the Alexa Magic

# By Ben Alexi

## Table of contents

# CHAPTER ONE: Understanding the High-Tech Amazon Eco Show

Amazon.com introduces smart speakers that come with different and more advanced experience with the Amazon products. The second-generation Echo speaker controlled by the Amazon's Alexa enhances its smart-home, digital-assistant abilities as well as the music expansion. The voice recognition feature of the high-tech speaker enables the user to command it to perform a number of operation from his or her comfort.

Ever since the introduction of the smart speaker in the year 2014 by the Amazon Lab126, the global population considers this device to enhance the livelihood of the modern homes. Customization of the product was also possible to enhance and personalize the experience of this technological intervention for a better experience. The installation of additional "skills" in the settings app is critical in improving the functionalities of the device.

Most users consider the Alexa products such as the Amazon Echo to provide real-time information that enhances their living standards. The weather and traffic information, for example, is critical for the owners of the Amazon products in planning their daily programs for a successful social, economic and political development. Professionals say the users activate the gadget verbally. A simple wake-up word like Echo is enough to enhance the productivity. However, the Amazon iOS, Android or the mobile apps require the consumer of the product to first activate the product to ensure that they get the best out of their investments.

On May 9, 2017, therefore, a new device Amazon Echo Show broke into the market with the aim of matching the advancing technology. The dealers within the United States unveiled it to the US market on June the same year. The Amazon Echo product with an additional 7-inch screen that is sensitive to touch received positive reviews upon its introduction into the market. Most experienced purchasers of this reasonable claim that the sound quality is relatively higher than to the preceding Amazon Echo releases. According to them, the screen supplements the workability of the Alexa. The product is available for the users within the United States, Germany, the

United Kingdom as well as Austria to expose them to all the benefits that come with the Alexa.

*The Amazon Echo Show*

The product comes with additional features, as an improvement of the first releases, to address the issues that arose from among the long-term users of the products with the intention of improving the lifestyle of the users while increasing the sales of the Alexa products in the process. The product includes the automatic Alexa skills that display the skill cards returned in the response objects. The ability to customize the product gives the user the feeling of ownership. Other benefits of the product, including reminding the users of important appointments on a special calendar. Other than being the first Amazon's Alexa-enabled gadget to have a screen, it is critical to understand the applicability of the features that come with the product.

Although the users have to dig deeper into their pockets, economists argue that the cost-benefit analysis indicates that the customers enjoy the value of their hard-earned cash.

Factors such as the cost of the products dictate the decision of the customer to choose the Alexa device that would enable them to upgrade their livelihood using the high-tech devices as their personal assistants.

Therefore, the customer needs to consider his or her reasons for the commodity such as their preferences or their financial stability. The multiple benefits of the Amazon Echo Show, therefore, make it a wise product to invest.

Unfortunately, this gadget comes with some negative features that discourage some clients from purchasing it. Its inability to support YouTube, for example, means that the most movie lovers would not prefer acquiring this revised model of the Amazon Echo line.

The user, having the facts at hand, decides on whether to purchase the product or not to. Despite the negative aspects of this gadget, the Amazon Echo Show comes with unique features that improve your experience when navigating through the screen of the gadget.

The next chapter, therefore, includes the specific features that make the product outstanding from among the Alexa commodities.

This guidebook, therefore, includes the many different chapters, with each explaining specific aspect of the product before a person opts to purchase the product.

Among the issues addressed in this book, including the defining features of this great improvement of the Amazon Echo Show, the systematic procedure for setting up the device as well as the specific commonly asked questions that the global users raise regarding the smart speaker.

The book also includes the common troubleshooting of the common technical issues experienced by the different users of the product to help the users mend the issues for a prolonged enjoyment of the product. Therefore, the users need to go through this comprehensive publication before trying to get the best out of their experience with the high-tech product.

# CHAPTER TWO: Why Purchase the Amazon Echo Show: Its Special Features

Just like the other Amazon Echo products, the introduction of the Amazon Echo shows aimed at exposing the users to an enhanced experience of the Alexa.

The gadget receives positive reviews since its first introduction into the market since it comes with unique features that enhance the experience of the users compared to that of the previous releases like the Amazon Echo Spot.

One of the significant difference of this gadget is the presence of a 7-inch touchscreen that displays the visual output of the Alexa responses.

Other than the touchscreen, the device has additional properties that make it unique as well as enhances its functionality.

This chapter, therefore, explains the significance of the outstanding features of this high-tech product of the Amazon Echo technology. Although this device is more expensive than the remaining Amazon Echo devices, its features make it a valuable purchase for the technology lovers.

### 1. Smart Home Skill API

This feature interprets the users' utterances to display the status of the configured devices in the Alexa app. The customer has the ability to view the video of his or her smart home through the cameras located on the Echo Show using this Smart Home Skill API.

Owners of these smart speakers have the ability to stream live the videos of their choices without having to create a voice interaction model for the camera skill.

This ability is because the Smart Home Skill API taps into the standardized Alexa language model of the product by the model.

The Alexa product understands the customers' utterances and then send the directives to the skills adapter that responds by resending the video feed from the camera requested by the customers from their comfort.

However, for this feature to work, the customer need to link it to their Amazon account with the device cloud to help discover the devices associated with the account.

In case the user needs to be sure that the child is asleep, he or she simply makes the statement "Alexa, show me the baby's room." Upon recognizing the voice, the Alexa sends the directives containing the clients' authentication data, the identifier for the devices as well as the new setting value.

This device sends an error message in case the customer is not authorized to view the cameras.

The security performance ensures that the confidential data is not displayed to the unauthorized persons through the cameras.

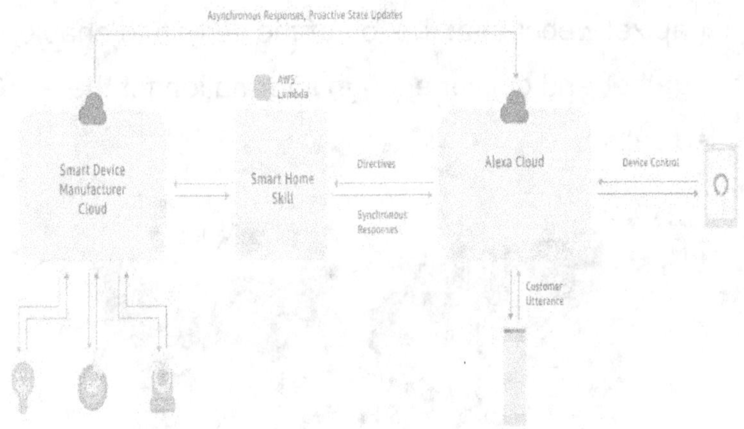


*A display of how the Smart Home Skill API work*

## 2. A 7-inch touchscreen

The presence of the screen to display the visual output for the Alexa assistant responses. The display is at 1,024 x 600 sharp making it clear and bright to display all the desired content by the customers. The owners of this special device claim that the screen looks aesthetic in the eyes and hence gives the house an aesthetic look.

The viewing angles of the screen are quite decent with enough contrast to enable the images to pop as well. The screen helps the users to enjoy many uses such as video calling due to the availability of the 5-megapixel webcam at the top of the screen to enable it to gather and deliver enough information for the video calls.

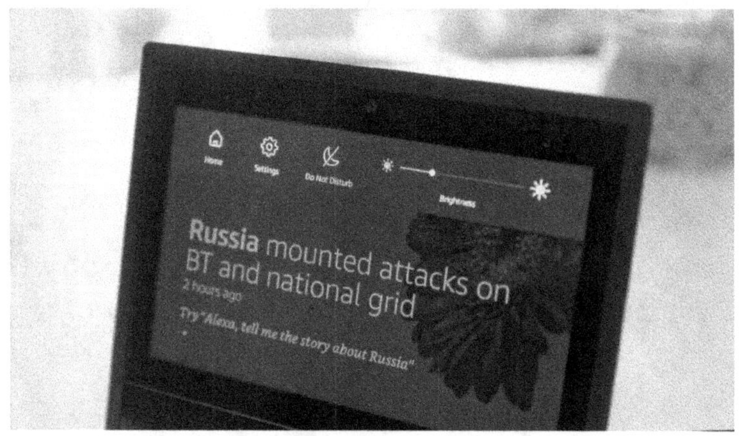


***The Amazon Echo Screen with a 5-megapixel webcam for video calling***

### 3. Excellent quality speakers

The 23.5cm Echo comes not only with the excellent screen but also with quality speakers to enhance the quality of sound produced by the devices. Below the screen is a flat grille that allows the device's twin 2in speaker drivers with the simple rear speakers. The two-2in stereo speaker produces quality sound compared to the Echo's 2.5in woofer or rather the 2in tweeter combo.

Other than the speakers, the gadget includes an extra microphone to receive the command before transmitting them through the system for conversion and conveyance to the owner.

Unfortunately, this gadget lacks the 360-degree sound as in the case of the preceding Echo products. Professionals, therefore, advise the users to place it near a wall or rather a corner to bring out its best quality sound.

*A flat grille to allow the 2in stereo speaker drivers*

**4. Three switches at the top of the screen**

The top of the screen, on the same note, includes three toggles that allow the users to either mute the microphones or rather adjust the volume. With the buttons, the users have full control of their purchase to be sure that they get the best out of their hard-earned cash.

*Three knobs at the top of the screen*

### 5.  The device comes with a YouTube feature

The Amazon, just like any other device with a screen, comes with the YouTube feature to allow the user to play the videos of their choice upon connecting the gadget to the internet. The earlier releases of those Echo products did not have the feature following the claim by Google that the device was using a substandard presentation of its product (the YouTube app).

Now Amazon Echo Show, with the help of the Voicebot, allows the users of this product to enjoy the YouTube upon browsing. This allowance makes it possible for them to be playing the videos, including the movies any time they connect their devices to the internet source.

Other than the YouTube feature, this latest Echo product includes the Dailymotion and the Vimeo video access hence enhances the experience of the owners that love to watch movies as a form of leisure.

The producers of this product claim that more video sources will be added to the future releases of the products to meet the desires of the target clients.

*A movie showing on the YouTube*

## Other features

The device, just like the other Echo products, lacks the built-in battery. This means that the batteries can be replaced with new ones in case they begin showing the signs of draining faster than normal.

However, it is advisable to consult the dealers of this device before opting to purchase the batteries for the Amazon Echo Show.

It is, therefore, critical for the user to maintain his or her Echo product to ensure that the rechargeable battery lasts long enough.

Unfortunately, this device lacks the 3.5mm analog output that is contained in the other Echo commodities.

For this reason, it is not possible for the owners to connect the Echo Show to the Hi-Fi for enhanced sound quality.

This is because it is believed that the product comes with the best quality sound that does not require any manipulation from the users.

The screen of the Amazon Echo Show displays a series of "cards" that changes at the count of seconds to display different information for the benefit of the users.

The news headlines, the time and the weather info, is the example of data contained in the cards. The cards also display suggestions for the user to make it easier for him or her to understand the device for memorable navigation throughout the seasons.

Upon the setting of alarms, the cards allow for the addition of new information at the will of the user.

# CHAPTER THREE: Setting up The Amazon Echo Show for the Beginners

Once you have sacrificed much to acquire this high-tech product, it is now time to begin enjoying your purchase. Some initial settings need to precede to enable the user access the outstanding properties that come with the product for an enhanced experience.



This chapter, therefore, entails all the information that aims at exposing the owner of this advanced technology to feel the value of their purchase. The info will range from the unboxing process to the advanced setting of the product.

## A. Unboxing the Amazon Echo Show

Now that you have your box of the Echo Show, you are required to open the package and get hold of the actual products that would transform you into a classier individual than many people residing within the universe. Other than the Amazon Echo Show, the package also contains a guiding pamphlet for the new users, both the adaptor and the power cord as well as guideline about the Alexa commands.

Download the companion Amazon Echo app on your IOS or the Android devices to allow the user customize different settings to match their preferred settings. Plug in the device into a power socket to begin the initial settings.

### B. Setting up the Amazon Echo Show

The first step after plugging the device is to select the language of your preference followed by keying in the Wi-Fi credentials to be sure that you can access the internet to continue with your set up the process.

Input your Amazon account data through navigating the screen because of the fact that the product can only be purchased by the Amazon prime members. Those individuals without the account cannot enjoy the features of this 2017 release.

Once you have logged in to your Amazon account, it is now advisable to begin the settings by linking all your applicable music services. To do this, the first step entails opening the **Amazon Alexa app** before heading to the **side menu** to select the **Music, Video,**

**& Books**. From this point, the user has the ability to select the specific songs he or she would wish to play on the Amazon Echo Show, including the Amazon music, the Amazon Music streaming service, Pandora, Spotify, Sirius XM, TuneIn and the iHeartRadio.

Although you need to be a subscriber to enjoy the properties, some of the choices like the Amazon Music and the TuneIn requires no subscription at all. Songs from the Amazon would include the lyrics to enable the user of this gadget sing with the artist. To turn this off, however, the user needs to just say a simple "**Alexa, turn on/off lyrics**."

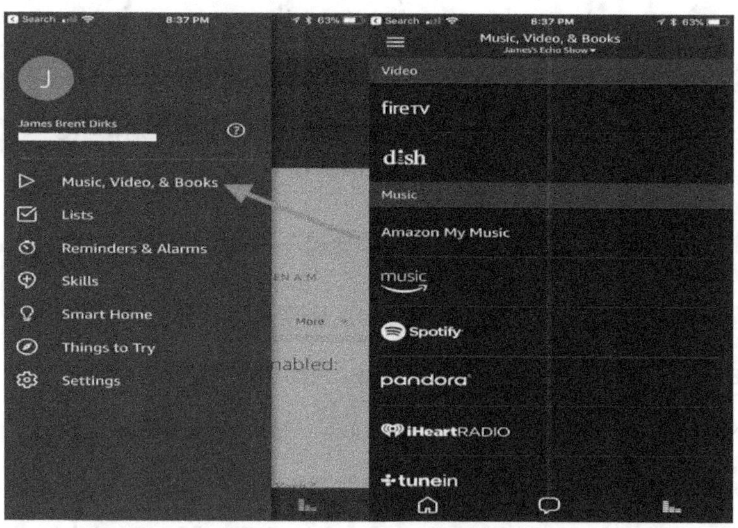

*Move to the sidebar and select the Music, Videos, & Books*

The three buttons at the top of the device allow the user to control the gadget. The one on the left-hand side is a Do Not Disturb button that is applicable in turning off both the camera and microphone when not in use.

The remaining two buttons, however, are used to control the volumes of the smart speakers with not Alexa command.

For an enhanced sound, the user might wish to connect the gadget to an external audio output, especially using the Bluetooth.

To enable this, the owner just says "**Alexa, go to Settings**" then simply select the **Bluetooth** before pairing the Bluetooth speaker you would wish to connect to your gadget. Once the pairing is done, follow the steps that follow. Alternatively, you can reach the **Settings** option by swiping down the screen.

## C. Setting the Household Profiles

The gadget might be for the household use. Such a scenario means that more than one uses will have access to the content of the device. Unfortunately, this would only be possible upon setting by the user. Every connected user will not only enjoy the features but also able to manage his or her music library once they consider the support of the Household Profiles features supported by the Echo Show.

From the app downloaded on either your iOS or Android device, head to the menu sidebar then choose the **Settings** followed by the **Account** and the **Household Profiles**.

From this point, the user will have to follow the instruction that would follow on the screen. The added persons have access to not only your Prime Photos on the Echo Show but also the Amazon account to allow them to make purchases as well as the ability to customize the news, music, shopping list among other privileges that come with the product.

In case you would desire to switch the accounts, you simply need to say "**Alexa, what account is this?**" followed by "**Alexa, switch accounts**."

For the users that would desire to remove an account, he or she would need to go to **Settings** followed by the **Accounts** then **In an Amazon household with [name]**. From this point, select the **Remove** option that is located next to the particular user you would wish to delete. However, in case you desire to remove yourself, simply click on the **Leave** option followed by the **Remove** to confirm the process.

***Note***: It is important for the users of this outstanding smart speaker to understand that the removed account can never be added back to any other household within a span of six months after the removal.

### D. Teaching Your Amazon Echo Show New Skills

Once the setup process is complete, it is now time to understand the more than 15,000 different skills that would enhance the experience of the users.

These skills are voice-controllable apps hence need the experience to get the best out of them. Although some of the skills are primarily designed for the preceding audio-only Echo products, some make use of the Echo Show screen to facilitate its functionality.

Unfortunately, it is still not easy to detect the skills that are optimized for the screens or those for the audio-versions.

The first step entails and enabling the skills.  To do this, there exist different strategies for the Echo Show users.

The best options to help in the identification of the skills to include in your device are found on the **Amazon Skills Portal**. However, the most convenient route to get the skills is using the companion app.

To use this app, you simply need to navigate from the side menu to locate the **<u>Skills</u>** option. From this point, you will see a list of trending skills to include in your device.

In case you are sure of the skill you desire, a search bar is located at the top of the page to help you locate it for easy adding into the Amazon Echo Show.

However, it is advisable to click on the Category icon located just next to the search bar. On every skill page, specific voice command, customer reviews, option to receive support concerning the skill as well as the description of the skill is some of the information that would help you select only the skills that meet your taste.

Upon identification of your skill of interest, simply click on the **Enable** button to enable it. Although some of the options would call for you to the first login to the companion service before enabling the skill, most of them just require the tapping of the **Enable** icon.

This process is much easier for the individuals who know the name of the skill they need to enable. Such a user simply needs to say "**Alexa, enable [skill name]**" and the skill will automatically enable itself.

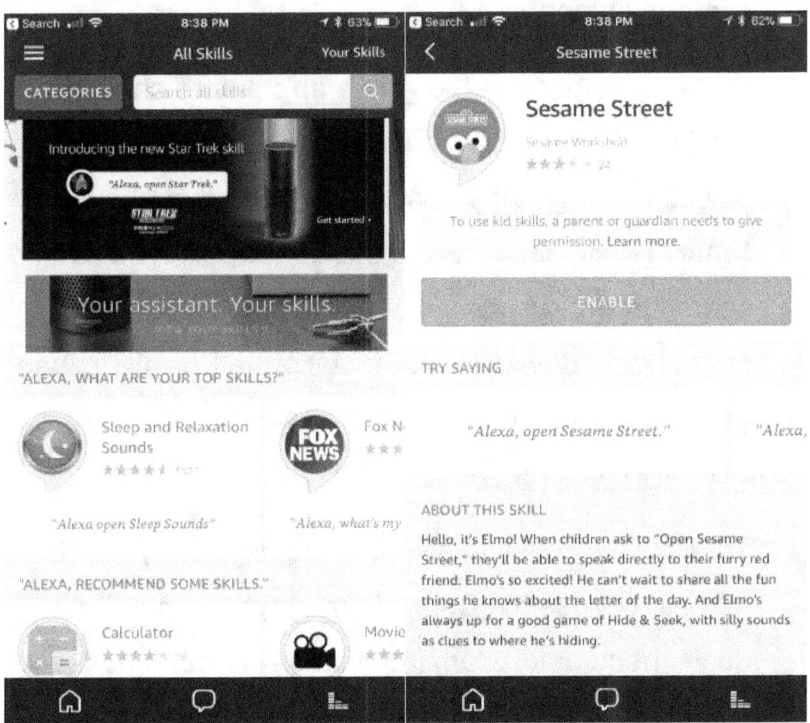

*Enabling the skills using the companion app*

During the selection of the skills, there exist different categories for the users to choose from, including the Food & Drink, Health & Fitness, Local, Lifestyle among several others depending on your personal interest.

The next step is to identify the smart home devices compatible with the Echo Show. Once you have identified the compatible smart home devices, you will be required to download the manufacturer's companion app.

From the app, open the **Alexa app** before choosing the **Smart Home** icon from the side menu before selecting the **Devices** and finally open the **Alexa Smart Home Store**. From this either point you can search or browse for the skills that correspond to the smart home device before tapping the **Enable** to lead you to the process that would allow you link your device with the service.

To allow the Alexa to discover the devices, you will need to choose the **Smart Home** option from the app's menu before tapping on the **Devices** and then **Discover**. Alternatively, you will need to simply say "**Alexa, discover devices**." From this point, the Alexa will display the number of devices detected or command the gadget to say the number of devices found.

In case, however, you need to remove a smart home device from the Echo Show, locate the **Smart Home** from the side menu before selecting the **Devices**. From this point, tap the **Forget** on each device to remove the selected devices. Deleting the device from the manufacturer's companion apps is advisable.

Upon the connection of the devices, however, you can simply control the processes using the simple voice command

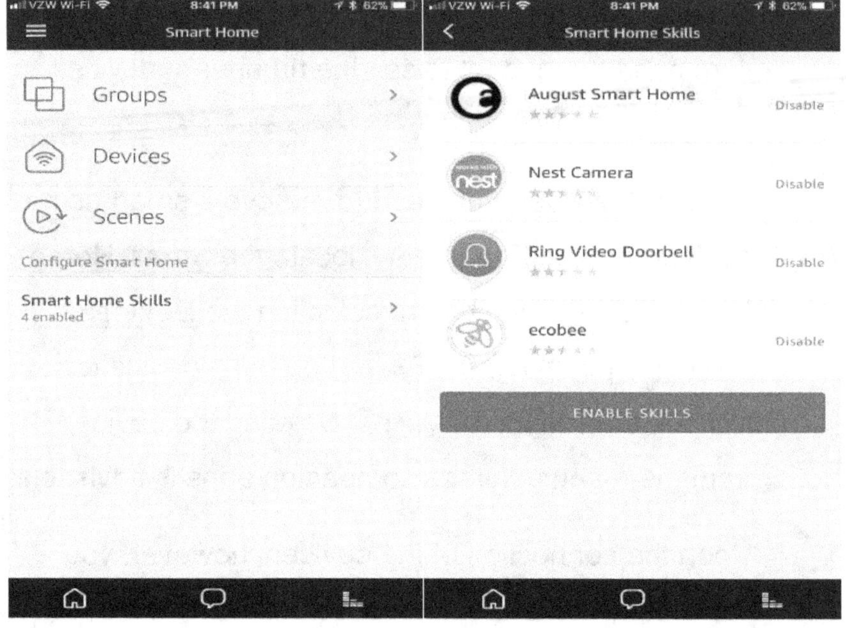

*A list of Smart Home Skills enabled*

## Special tips to make use of the Echo Show

> ➢ You have the ability to change the Wake Word using your Alexa App installed on your PC or the mobile device. To do this, simply go to **Settings** then choose the **Echo Show as your device**. From this point, scroll down o the **Wake Word** option before making your choice of word. Confirm the process by tapping on the **Save** option.

- ➤ From this point, you will be able to converse with your Echo device through ***asking questions*** or rather ***giving commands***. Upon recognizing the question, this device responds verbally. Alternatively, the device can respond by displaying the results or automatically perform the task commanded by the user.
- ➤ The user has to talk to the device in natural tones at a normal pace. Continuous use of the natural tones will let the Echo device familiar with the speech patterns.
- ➤ The tapping pressure used when using the smartphones is the same intensity that the user needs to apply when using the touchscreen of the Echo Show gadget.
- ➤ The user can control the Alexa device using the smartphone or rather the tablet even when far from home.
- ➤ The user has the ability to sample his or her favorite skills such as Playing Music, Make a Phone Call as well as Watching Videos.

Therefore, the next chapter of this book includes the memorable skills that would enhance the experience of the individual users. It is, therefore, critical for the first time users to navigate through the content of the following chapter in order to get the best experience of the high-tech product ever.

# CHAPTER FOUR: Application of the Amazon Echo Show

Enabling skills in your Amazon Echo Show enhances aim at facilitating the experience of the user. This statement means that the skills dictate the functionalities of the device based on the customization of the user.

More than 5,000 skills are available for the Echo Show owners. It is impossible for the lovers of this Echo product to enable all the skills and hence the need to select the ones they feel would be of benefit to them throughout their season of possessing this outstanding gadget.

This section of the book, therefore, select the best skills that make the user have a memorable experience as well as maintaining their place at the top of the pyramid.

I. **The device allows you to shop for the goods of your choice**

The advancing technology has forced the business people to venture into online trades. This consideration follows the fact that most of the global population use the internet on their everyday operations. The product and service consumers order their products from the comfort of their homes before the online companies organize themselves for swift delivery.

Amazon is not left behind following the introduction of the new Echo Show device that allows the users to order for their products. The camera included in the device allows you to scan the product before ordering them.

To do the scanning, hold the product's barcode facing the camera then say "**Alexa, scan**." Upon the recognition of the product, the screen will display the option to make an order for the product.

The Amazon prime members have the privilege of using the voice command feature to search for the products they need to purchase from Amazon. They simply tell Alexa what they desire to buy.

**A Skippy Cream ordered online**

## II.    The user can call an Uber using the device

Commuting has been made easy with the introduction of Uber. This transport service allows you to order from your doorstep in case you are late for an important meeting.

However, you risk missing your Uber when putting your coat on without having your focus on the phone.

For this reason, Amazon introduced an outstanding Echo Show that will prevent you from missing the Uber services. You simply need to enable the Uber skill on your device to begin enjoying the service via your Echo Show. The owners of this outstanding

Echo product have the choice of selecting the car service they desire as well as determine the specific person coming to pick them up. You will know that the Uber has arrived without having to pull out your phone.

### III.    The ability to monitor your home

Smart homes consider using the smart home cameras to have full control of the happening within the premise. As the owner of this outstanding gadget, you are required to link the smart camera to your Echo Show and use it to monitor what is happening around all the corner of your house.

Women enjoy this skill when in the kitchen but still watching their children in the bedrooms. The ability of the user to watch a feed from the from his or her smart security camera ensures that an intruder does not have access to any corner of the premise. Other than the security camera, this Echo Show has the ability to command a wide variety of the smart-home devices that would ensure that you get the best out of your hard-earned cash investment.

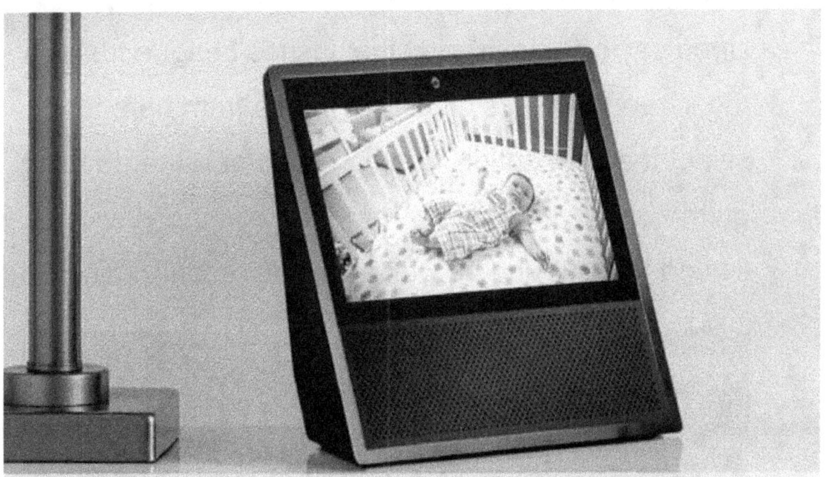

*The display of a child in the bedroom on the Echo Show screen*

IV. **The ability to watch videos using the gadget**

Everyone desire to watch the trailer for the latest movie release. People crowd the internet to at least have a taste of what to expect when watching the entire movie. This experience, therefore, is made easy following the decision of the Amazon to release the 2017 Amazon Echo Show device.

The users of this proof of enhanced technology can have the preview of the shootings through a mere voice command.

Upon saying "Alexa, play the Justice League trailer," the screen displays different options from here to select the best option via your voice or rather tapping on the displayed option. Unfortunately, this device is limited to YouTube as well as the Amazon Video.

***The Justice League trailer on the Echo Sound touchscreen.***

## V.  The device acts as an assistant in the kitchen

This device can provide the best cooking options to ensure that you prepare delicious meals for both your family members and guests.

Whichever recipe you would wish to prepare is available on the touchscreen of this excellent Amazon production. The owner of the device simply needs to say the recipe he or she desires to prepare, and the procedure will display on the screen for fast preparation.

In circumstances where the user needs to prepare a pumpkin dish, he or she simply says, "**<u>Alexa, find me the recipes for pumpkin pie</u>**" and the gadget automatically displays the results for an enhanced cooking experience.

***A displayed pumpkin pie recipes on the Echo
Show screen***

## VI.    The users of this product can make video calls.

The ability to make video calls has made this device a hot cake in the market. The user of this Amazon commodity has the ability to video chat with any other friend with the Echo show or rather the Alexa app on their handsets or the PC.

A drop in feature does not require the user to turn the camera on when receiving the video calls. The contacts simply drop on the Echo Show before automatically making the calls.

Unfortunately, the fact that you do not have to grant permission for the contacts to drop in means has earned this product some negative reviews from the customers. Another issue is the fact that the person you need to call has to be in your contact list for you to make the calls.

*The Echo Show allows you to connect through the video chat*

## VII.    The users have the ability to catch up on the latest news

Every person desire to be up to date with the latest news feed. For this reason, people spend most of their time online trying to keep the trending news.

Amazon has made it much easier for the users to access the latest news through different ways. When the Echo Show is idling, the top news headlines display on the touchscreen.

Upon noticing a headline that interests you, you need to simply ask the Alexa feature for more information about the topic. The gadget responds by giving a synopsis of the happenings regarding your question of interest.

In fact, Alexa will read the summary aloud for you to keep updated. Alternatively, other users prefer clicking on the screen to open the newsfeed rather than having it read aloud by the smart speaker.

Fortunately, enabling either the USA Today skill or the CNN skill will feed you with both the regional and international news. The two skills include five rundown videos daily regarding the top five stories that hit the headline that particular day.

***The user has the ability to access the latest news using the Echo Show.***

Other than the above-explained application of the Amazon Echo Show, acquiring this product exposes the user to several additional experiences that enhance their lifestyle. The ability to control the home entertainment, the workout guide, and the calendar are some of the examples of this outstanding product of the Amazon Company.

# CHAPTER FIVE: The Timesaving Tricks and Tips to Get the Best Out Of Amazon Echo Show

The introduction of the Amazon Echo Show allows the user to have control over his or her smart home devices. Although the experience is memorable, you might need to adjust or rather customize your Echo Show for a personalized and excellent experience.

This chapter, therefore, includes some of the best tricks and tips that will help you get the best out of your valuable gadget. The additional settings will help you enjoy the specific skills that you have selected and enabled on your device. Going through the content if this section will enable you to have a clue on what to do in order to enjoy the skills.

## 1. Customizing the Drop In

This Echo Show product enables other people with the device to be able to control your gadget without having to approve the item. Although this seems like exposing your data to unauthorized users, you have the power to decide the people that Drop In on your device.

The selected persons will have the ability to start a video or audio at their will. The users of this Echo product use their phones to readjust the list of the people with the privilege to Drop In. This selection is made via the Alexa app that is already installed on your handset.

From the app, locate the **Settings** followed by the **Echo Show**. From this point, you will be able to see a list of devices. Choose the **Drop-In** option. A display with three options appears: **On**, **Only my household** and **Off**. Choose the option you desire from the three. Turning on the Drop-In will force you to select the Alexa contacts you would wish to access your data.

To do this, therefore, choose the **Conversation tab** located at the bottom of the Alexa app then select the **contact icon** at the top of the screen. Select the contacts of your choice before tapping the **Contact can Drop-In at anytime** option. Selecting the **Only, my household** option will only allow those within your household to use their devices to Drop In.

2. **Customize your background photo**

The default Amazon background photo might be boring to you. That should not worry you since there is an option to upload the picture of your choice to give an excellent background.

You simply need to have access to the Alexa app on your phone. Locate the Settings for your Show then navigate downwards to locate a blue button that is labeled **Choose A Photo**. From this point, select your best photo from the camera roll, crop it and upload it to your customized background.

### 3.  Sound controls

The sound of your alarm or the notification might be either too loud or low. Amazon Echo Show comes with the features that enable you to adjust the volume to your desired level. On your Amazon Echo Show, visit the **Settings** then the **Sounds** to complete the adjustment. You will also be able to adjust the start/end request sound.

### 4.  Taking pictures using the Echo Show

You might decide to either take a simple photo or rather a group photo. The Echo Show is a good device to help you with this. To do this, simply tell

Alexa to take the picture. A camera app with three different camera options displays forcing you to tap on the one you desire. Alternatively, you can tell Alexa the number of cameras you wish to use. Position yourself to take the best snap for future reference.

### 5.  Go home, Alexa

You might be enjoying a skill and feel as if you need to go back to the home screen. Simply say "Alexa, go home," and it will automatically go back. Alternatively, you can decide to swipe from the top of the Echo Show display than simply tap the **Home** icon.

### 6.  Set up the Do Not Disturb (DND)

You might be enjoying your skills before an annoying message, call, or a new skill alert interrupts you. This device has you covered. The only thing you are required to do is to enable the Do Not Disturb icon on your Echo Show. On your Echo Show, swipe down from the screen top to display an on-demand button to help you to turn the DND either on or off.

Fortunately, it is also possible to schedule the feature to turn on or off automatically. To do this, swipe on the Echo Show to display the menu. From this point, locate the **Settings** then scroll downwards to identify the **Do Not Disturb** option to customize your schedule.

### 7. Alexa will help you set reminders

Organized people have a schedule to ensure they execute their responsibilities diligently. Some of them note down the specific events that they need to attend in future.

Unfortunately, most of them forget or sometimes lose the material on which they had noted the dates for reference. The Echo Show, however, make this an easy task to ensure that you do not miss your appointment or even a class. You simply need to tell Alexa to remind you of the event when the time arrives. When the time comes, your device will light up and remind you to keep time for the event.

### 8. Do some quick maths on your device

Some device has their calculator app hidden in a folder. It becomes difficult and timewasting to locate it. With the Echo Show, however, you simply need to ask Alexa to help you with the summation. In case you need to find 10% of 653, simply say "**<u>Alexa, what is 10% of 653.</u>**" An instant answer follows.

### 9. Muting your Echo Show

There come times when you require privacy to think over your plans with the aim of seeing them through. During such times, the device's wake words are irritating hence the need to mute your gadget to allow you continue with your meditation.

To do this, therefore, simply push the left button at the top of the device (it is slashed through the microphone). A red ring displays to show that the gadget is muted. Repressing the button turns the device on once again.

# CHAPTER SIX: The Common Amazon Echo Show Troubleshooting Strategies

The Amazon Echo Show has realized tremendous success ever since its introduction into the market. Studies predict that it will continue hitting the market for more years to come.

Despite having the power to enhance the experience of the users, the experienced users of this special Echo release reported some issues that undermine the navigation success of the user through the outstanding skills that are enabled in their Echo Show.

This chapter, therefore, highlights some of the commonly reported issues of this excellent invention.

## 1) The Echo Show won't power on

In case the device fails to power on, the electronic specialists argue that the problem can be either a faulty motherboard or power adapter in the case of a faulty adapter, for example, it is advisable to purchase a new one to continue enjoying the goodies that come with this commodity. For the faulty motherboard, you as well need to replace it.

### 2) A frozen screen

Your screen might fail to respond to the input due to two different reasons, including a dirty screen and a faulty circuit board. It is, therefore, critical to identify the reason for the occurrence of the issue before opting to the specific interventions to rectify the situation.

Use a clean and soft cloth or rather the designated screen cleaners to wipe the dirt on the screen, including the screen edges.

The failure of the screen to respond is because of the effects of the dust that blocks the LED lights known to boarder the screen. With the soft clothing, however, it is possible to remove the dirt and continue enjoying the value of your hard-earned cash. For a faulty circuit board, on the other hand, it is advisable to replace it with a functional one.

However, in case, none of the above is the reason for the disappointment, it is advisable to restart the device to get it begin functioning. To do this, you first need to unplug the Echo Show from the charging source then reboot by long pressing the power button for approximately a half a minute.

### 3) My Echo Show is not connecting to the Wi-Fi

There comes a time when your device refuses to connect to the local network available. This can result due to the problem with your router or modem.

To rectify this, therefore, you will have to turn off your Echo Show first followed by switching off the router or rather the modem. Wait for approximately 30 seconds before turning on the router or modem on. From this point, try to connect your gadget through. In case the problem persists, then your service provider might be having some technical issues affecting your experience.

The availability of the dead pixel (line on the screen)

Your screen might display certain unaesthetic lines making it challenging to enjoy your valuable gadget. This issue can be a result of interference for the foreign devices or a faulty screen.

In case the cause is placing it next to stronger devices like the computer or rather a printer, move the gadget away from the devices.

Reboot your Echo Show by long pressing the power button for about 30 seconds to rectify the error. However, in case the issues are because of the screen being faulty, it is advisable to replace it with a new and functional one.

### 4) Alexa won't connect to my Bluetooth devices

This device includes both the Audio/Video Remote Control Profile (AVRCP) and the Advanced Audio Distribution Profile (A2DP SNK) to determine the compatibility of the device you are about to connect. However, your device might fail to connect to the Bluetooth gadget.

In this case, therefore, you will need to un-pair and then re-pair your Bluetooth devices. To do this, therefore, open the Alexa app then open the Settings. From your Echo device locate and select the Bluetooth option. From this point, clear all the paired devices.

To re-pair the device, on the other hand, you will need to put your Echo device in discoverable mode first by simply saying "Alexa, pair." From your device, locate the Bluetooth settings or the Alexa app to help you pair your devices.

### 5)  The Alexa skills are not playing up

The manufacturers of the Echo products claim that there exist up to 25,000 skills for the user to select the best skills to enable in his or her Echo Show. Although all of them are outstanding, some of them might seem to do contrary to how you direct them to. This failure can be either because your gadget is not a quality one.

However, some of such issues would simply require you to disable and re-able the product to boost your gadgets' performances. To disable the skill, use the Alexa app to Disable the Skills completely before re-enabling it. Upon the completion, restart your Amazon Echo Show to continue enjoying the excellent and memorable experience.

Before opting to disable and re-enable the skills, visit the Alexa app and browse to Your Skills. From here locate the Skill not working then navigate through the

Manage Preferences. This follows the tapping them on and off to see whether the problems will be resolved.

## 6)  Alexa does not understand me

Among the many reasons, why people prefer going for the Echo Show is the ability to voice-command it to get things done. Unfortunately, there comes a time when the device fails to respond to your command. It is obvious that you feel disappointed. Right! This is a common issue for the new devices. Your Echo Show will get to understand you with time.

It is, therefore, critical for the user to consider the voice-training tool to help rectify the problem. To do this, navigate through your Alexa app to **Settings** then identify the **Voice training**. From this point, you will be required to speak your 25 pre-selected phrases to help the device learn your lexicon.

Navigate to the app's Settings then tap the History to help you identify the word that your Alexa heard. From this point, you will be able to identify the misheard words to express them more clearly for Alexa to learn swiftly.

If all the correctional strategies fail, the last option is to perform a factory reset on your Amazon Echo Show to give it a fresh start. To do this, therefore, locate the reset button located next to the power adapter. Use a pin to hold the button until the light rings turn orange. Unfortunately, once done, you will be required to set up the Echo Show all over again.

# CHAPTER SEVEN: The Commonly Asked Questions about the Amazon Echo Show.

The long-time users of this device can confirm the significance of this great device. They have been able to enjoy their excellent skills through the memorable navigation through the devices. New timers, however, take time to understand how this device operates.

However, the 24/7 Amazon support center has proven to be reliable for them. They are allowed to ask any question regarding the use of the Amazon Echo Show. The competent Amazon staff provides them with all the responses to enhance their experience.

This chapter, therefore, select some of the commonly asked questions. Understanding these issues would not only help the users understand how the Echo Show operated but also the Amazon staff due to the reducing of their workload.

### a) How do I use Alexa?

Alexa is a cloud service of the Amazon that works differently depending on the Alexa-based product. For the Echo Show product, however, you activate Alexa by simply saying the Wake Word or rather the power button. In case you need anything done, you simply ask Alexa, and it will be done. In case you want to add a skill, say "**Alexa, enable [skill name]**."

### b) Will the voice service improve with time?

Alexa requires training to understand your commands. The quality of the voice and response will improve with time. Use the training tool from the settings to let your device get better for an enhanced experience.

### c) How do Alexa skills work?

Skills are defined as the voice-driven words that make it easier for the owners of these excellent products feel their value. Upon enabling a skill, use them by simply saying specific phrases depending on the skill that you are using. If you need to take a camera, for example, you simply say "**Alexa, take a picture**" and it takes your best snap.

### d) What are the return order policies for the goods I order using the Alexa?

The people that order the non-digital products enjoy the free returns. To do this using the Alexa, simply process the return as normal in the Amazon's Return Center. In case you use the Alexa to request for the products, visit Amazon's About Our Returns Policies to understand the return policies of the products you request.

### e) How does the Alexa work with the smart home devices?

Alexa will allow you to control the status of the smart home devices like the outlets, lights, thermostats among several others. The first step entails identifying the smart devices that are compatible with your Echo Show. Use the Alexa smart home skills to connect the compatible home gadgets to the Alexa. From here, you simply need to voice-command Alexa to help you check the status of the smart home devices.

### f) What is a recently active indicator?

This is a sign indicating whether there is someone near your supported Echo devices. This active indicator displays only on the Echo Show of the people granted Drop In.

### g)  How do I disable the Drop In?

Once you have granted your household members the privilege to Drop In anytime, you can disable them on your contact card. In case you did give the privilege to any other contact, you disable them on their contact cards. You also have the ability to disable Drop In for a specific device through the device settings found in the Alexa app on your phone.

### h)  What is Do Not Disturb?

The Do Not Disturb feature allows your device to be in a silent mode to enable you to have quality time to meditate. You will not be able to receive either calls or messages through your Alexa. To do this, simply say "Alexa, turn on the do not disturb." Alternatively, you can go to Settings in your Alexa app to enable the skill.

### i)  Who will receive my calls and messages?

Every person with the contact and whose device the Echo Show device supports will be able to access your messages and calls.

### j)  How do I remove the messages from my conversation list?

This process depends on your phone's operating system. For the Android version of the Alexa app, simply long press the conversation to choose it before tapping the trash icon located at the top of the navigation bar. For the iOS, however, swipe the conversation to the left followed by simple clicking on the "**<u>Remove</u>**" option to delete it.

### k) Can I call the emergency services using the Alexa calling and messaging?

No, you are not able to reach the emergency services like the 112 or the 999. You, therefore, need to ensure that you are able to access either a landline telephone, mobile or any other service in case of an emergency.

New users of this product, therefore, need to go through this chapter to get the responses to some of the commonly asked questions by the experienced users. This will ensure that they begin enjoying their valuable purchase from the word goes.

# Conclusion

Amazon has never disappointed its customers. The company introduced the Alexa, an Amazon's cloud-based voice service that is available on more than ten million devices produced by Amazon as well as the third-party devices producers.

The users have been able to build natural voice experiences to offer the customers a more intuitive way to enjoy the value of technology.

The company introduced new products like the Amazon Echo Show that are compatible with the Alexa service.

The Echo Show, just like the other Echo products, enhances voice interaction, making to-do lists, setting alarms among other important features.

The features are described as skills. Although there are more than 25,000 skills, the users need to select the best skills to enable on their Echo device and hence make use of the Alexa to control them.

Unlike the other Echo products, this Echo Show includes a touchscreen that ensures that it has additional properties than the rest of the products.

Understanding the defining features of this great device is critical for the Echo lovers to consider purchasing the Echo Show over the rest.

This book entails the systematic steps followed when enabling the skills on your gadgets, including the strategies used to enjoy each of the skills.

The special tricks and tips that would ensure that you get the best out of the skills are also included in the book. The many skills available means that the product has many applications that are valuable to the user.

Following the privilege of the consumers to review the Amazon products, this book has been able to highlight some of the critical issues that arise from the reviews.

The common troubleshooting of this Echo device ensures that the user is able to identify a problem with the product and then know the steps to consider rectifying the issues. The commonly asked questions are also included to provide guidance for the new users of this outstanding Amazon Echo product.

With all the information therein, it is critical for you to consider acquiring this outstanding book to ensure that you don't miss any of the valuable skills. Get your copy today and join the high-class people through the purchase of the Amazon Echo Show product.

## Other Books by Ben Alexi

Amazon
Prime
How to Make the Most Out of the Many Benefits
of Amazon Prime Membership
amazon Prime
BEN ALEXI

AMAZON
ECHO
EASY TO USE AMAZON ECHO GUIDE
BEN ALEXI

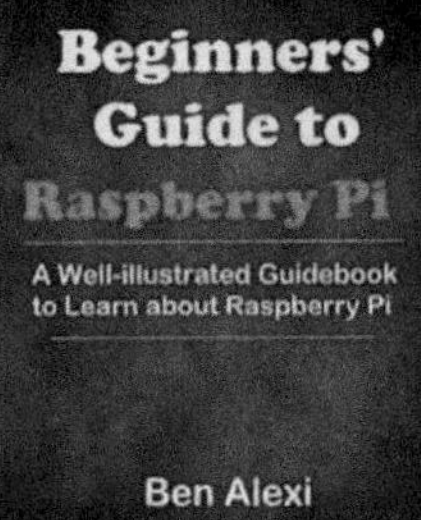
Beginners'
Guide to
Raspberry Pi
A Well-illustrated Guidebook
to Learn about Raspberry Pi
Ben Alexi

iPhone
7 and 7 Plus
A Detailed and Easy-to-Use
iPhone 7 and 7 Plus Book Guide
Ben Alexi

Self
Publishing
Step-by-Step
How to Publish Your Book
Using Amazon and Other
Platforms
2017
Ben Alexi

Galaxy S8
User Guide
An Easy Step-by-Step
Guide for Galaxy S8
Ben Alexi